CLIMB the Summer Slide 2nd level

Climb the Summer Slide

Read

Poor Tired Tim! It's sad for him.
He lags the long bright morning through,
Ever so tired of nothing to do;
He moons and mopes the livelong day,
Nothing to think about, nothing to say;
Up to bed with his candle to creep,
Too tired to yawn, too tired to sleep:
Poor Tired Tim! It's sad for him.

Copy the sentence below. Then add a rhyme. It doesn't have to make any sense. (Poor Tired Tim!)

_____

_____

Language Arts

Give each one-word sentence different ending punctuation.

Yeah　　　What　　　Okay

Math

$7 + 5 =$ 　　　　　　　$3 + 8 =$

$9 - 2 =$ 　　　　　　　$15 - 6 =$

What's next in the pattern? Draw the shape.

Read

I know a little cupboard,
With a teeny tiny key,
And there's a jar of Lollypops
For me, me, me.

What do you want? Write it and then finish with the line from the end of the poem. (...for me, me, me.)

_____

_____

Language Arts

Underline the two pronouns in the sentence.

I thanked him for the present.

Math

6 + 4 =   8 + 5 =

10 − 7 =   8 − 4 =

What time is it?

 _____

Read

Jimmy Skunk scratched his head thoughtfully as he watched Old Mr. Toad go down the Lone Little Path, hop, hop, hipperty-hop, towards the Smiling Pool. He certainly was puzzled, was Jimmy Skunk. If Old Mr. Toad had told him that he could fly, Jimmy would not have been more surprised, or found it harder to believe than that Old Mr. Toad had a beautiful voice. The truth is, Jimmy didn't believe it. He thought that Old Mr. Toad was trying to fool him.

Write the sentence. (I wouldn't believe it if someone told me that...**Finish it!**)

_____

_____

_____

Language Arts

Circle the action verbs.

dream   sleep   is   was   run

Math

$9 + 3 =$ $4 + 7 =$

$12 - 4 =$ $16 - 9 =$

Write the fraction, five sixths.

Climb the Summer Slide

Read

And even as they looked, his throat began to swell and swell and swell, until it was no wonder that Jimmy Skunk had thought that he was in danger of blowing up. And then, when it stopped swelling, there came again those beautiful little notes, so sweet and tremulous that Peter actually held his breath to listen. There was no doubt that Old Mr. Toad was singing just as he had said he was going to, and it was just as true that his song was one of the sweetest if not the sweetest of all the chorus from and around the Smiling Pool.

Write five words that rhyme with swell.

_____

_____

Language Arts

Which of these words ends in an S when plural? (bike, bike<u>s</u>)

man   sheep   child   dog

Math

8 + 5 =   9 + 4 =

13 – 4 =   11 – 3 =

How much money do you have?

     _____

Let's countdown 40, 39, 38, 37...

Read

Peter Rabbit had known for a long time about the Frog babies, but though he knew that Old Mr. Toad was own cousin to Grandfather Frog, he hadn't known anything about Toad babies, except that at a certain time in the year he was forever running across tiny Toads, especially on rainy days, and each little Toad was just like Old Mr. Toad, except for his size. Peter had heard it said that Toads rain down from the sky, and sometimes it seems as if this must be so. Of course he knew it couldn't be, but it puzzled him a great deal.

What puzzles you? Be curious and write a question. Why does...?

_____

_____

Language Arts

What's wrong with the sentence? Find three things.

whats wrong with this sentence.

Math

60 + 70 =   9 + 5 =

17 − 8 =   10 − 3 =

What's next in the pattern? Draw the shape.

      _____

Let's countdown 40, 39, 38, 37, 36...

Read

If you don't believe it, just you go ask Old Mr. Toad, as Peter Rabbit did, how such a slow-moving fellow as he is can catch enough bugs and insects to keep him alive. Perhaps you'll learn something just as Peter did. Peter and Old Mr. Toad sat in the rain watching the tiny Toads, who, you know, were Mr. Toad's children, leaving their kindergarten in the Smiling Pool and starting out to see the Great World. When the last little Toad had passed them, Old Mr. Toad suddenly remembered that he was hungry, very hungry indeed.

Copy the sentence. (If you don't believe it, just you go ask Old. Mr. Toad.)

_____

_____

Language Arts

Circle the letters that should be capitalized.

i'd like to visit alaska in june.

Math

8 + 7 =   6 + 9 =

16 – 8 =   15 – 7 =

What time is it?

_____

Let's countdown 40, 39, 38, 37, 36, 35...

Read

It was too much for Peter. Look as he would, he couldn't see so much as a chip under which Old Mr. Toad might have hidden, excepting the old board, and Old Mr. Toad had given his word of honor that he wouldn't hide under that. Nevertheless, Peter hopped over to it and turned it over again, because he couldn't think of any other place to look. Of course, Old Mr. Toad wasn't there. Of course not. He had given his word that he wouldn't hide there, and he always lives up to his word. Peter should have known better than to have looked there.

Finish the sentence. (If I could hide anywhere, I would hide...)

_____

_____

Language Arts

Write the contraction. Example: I am = I'm

He is _____

Math

4 + 8 =   7 + 5 =

15 − 8 =   13 − 5 =

Write the fraction shown by the picture.

Let's countdown 40, 39, 38, 37, 36, 35, 34...

Read

But there was no way to escape, and after a little Old Mr. Toad thought it best to be polite, because, you know, it always pays to be polite. So he said in a very faint voice that he would be pleased to dine with Buster. Then he waved his feet feebly, trying to get on his feet again. Buster Bear laughed harder than ever. It was a low, deep, grumbly-rumbly laugh, and sent cold shivers all over poor Old Mr. Toad. But when Buster reached out a great paw with great cruel-looking claws Mr. Toad quite gave up. He didn't have strength enough left to even kick. He just closed his eyes and waited for the end.

Copy the sentence. (There was no way to escape.)

_____

_____

Language Arts

Write the plural.

toy _____   cry _____

Math

60 + 60 =   7 + 4 =

18 − 9 =   12 − 5 =

How many pennies do you need to make a dollar?

_____

Let's countdown 40, 39, 38, 37, 36, 35, 34, 33...

Read

Old Mr. Toad didn't wait to be told twice. He forgot all about his fright. He forgot all about Buster Bear. He forgot that he wasn't hungry. He forgot his manners. He jumped right in among those ants, and for a little while he was the busiest Toad ever seen. Buster Bear was busy too. He swept his long tongue this way, and he swept it that way, and each time he drew it back into his mouth, it was covered with ants. At last Old Mr. Toad couldn't hold another ant. Then he remembered Buster Bear and looked up a little fearfully. Buster was smacking his lips, and there was a twinkle in each eye.

What were they eating? According to the last sentence, was Buster happy about it?

Language Arts

What's wrong with the sentence? Find four things.

pleas dont do that now?

Math

$8 + 8 =$ $3 + 7 =$

$14 - 7 =$ $12 - 4 =$

What's next in the pattern? Write the number.

1, 2, 4, 8, 16, 32... _____

Let's countdown 40, 39, 38, 37, 36, 35, 34, 33, 32...

Read

When Old Mr. Toad saw Mr. Blacksnake and turned his back on Buster Bear and the fine dinner to which Buster had invited him, he had but just one idea in his head, and that was to get out of sight of Mr. Blacksnake as soon as possible. He forgot to ask Buster Bear to excuse him. He forgot that he was tired and hot. He forgot all the pride with which he had been so puffed up. He forgot everything but the need of getting out of sight of Mr. Blacksnake as soon as ever he could.

What would you run away from? (I would run away from...) Make it as real or as silly as you like.

_____

_____

Language Arts

Circle the five letters that should be capitalized.

dr. martin luther king jr. was a preacher.

Math

5 + 8 =   6 + 4 =

15 − 9 =   16 − 7 =

What time is it?

   _____

Let's countdown 40, 39, 38, 37, 36, 35, 34, 33, 32, 31...

Climb the Summer Slide

Read

"Old Mr. Toad is a jolly good fellow!
His temper is sweet, disposition is mellow!
And now that his bubble of pride is quite busted
We know that he knows that his friends can be trusted."

Write a word that rhymes with fellow and mellow and a word that rhymes with busted and trusted.

Language Arts

What does the contraction mean?

he'll _____ don't _____

Math

50 + 80 =   7 + 9 =

15 – 9 =   13 – 8 =

Write the fraction shown by the picture.

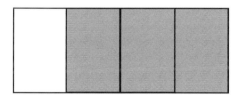

Read

That is why so many people are forever getting into trouble. He won't keep still. No, Sir, he won't keep still unless he is made to. Once let him get started there is no knowing where he will stop. Peter Rabbit had just seen Jimmy Skunk disappear inside an old barrel, lying on its side at the top of the hill, and at once the Imp of Mischief began to whisper to Peter. Of course Peter shouldn't have listened. Certainly not. But he did. You know Peter dearly loves a joke when it is on someone else. He sat right where he was and watched to see if Jimmy would come out of the barrel. Jimmy didn't come out, and after a little Peter stole over to the barrel and peeped inside. There was Jimmy Skunk curled up for a nap.

Copy the sentence. (Jimmy curled up for a nap.)

_____

Language Arts

Write the plural.

book _____   box _____

Math

$8 + 8 =$ $4 + 7 =$

$12 - 7 =$ $14 - 5 =$

How many nickels do you need to make one dollar? (Hint: 100 cents = $1)

 _____

Read

To sneak away is to steal away trying to keep out of sight of everybody, and is usually done only by those who for some reason or other are ashamed to be seen. Just as soon as Reddy Fox could see after Jimmy Skunk had thrown that terrible perfume in Reddy's face he started for the Green Forest. He wanted to get away by himself. But he didn't trot with his head up and his big plumey tail carried proudly as is usual with him. No indeed. Instead he hung his head, and his handsome tail was dropped between his legs; he was the very picture of shame. You see that terrible perfume which Jimmy Skunk had thrown at him clung to his red coat and he knew that he couldn't get rid of it, not for a long time anyway.

Answer the question. (Why was Reddy Fox's tail between his legs?)

Language Arts

What's wrong with the sentence? Find two things.

Doing chores teach's me to be a good worker

Math

56 + 90 =   7 + 3 =

12 − 5 =   14 − 8 =

What's next in the pattern? Write the number.

3, 6, 9, 12, 15, 18, 21, 24, 27, 30, 33, _____

Let's countdown 30, 29, 28...

Read

"It wouldn't be so bad if I had really been to blame, but I wasn't. I didn't know Jimmy Skunk was in that barrel and I didn't mean to start it rolling down the hill anyway," he muttered. "It was all an accident and " He stopped and into his yellow eyes crept a look of suspicion. "I wonder," said he slowly, "if Peter Rabbit knew that Jimmy Skunk was there and planned to get me into all this trouble. I wonder."

Put the sentence in order. (. planned all trouble Jimmy Skunk this)

_____

_____

Language Arts

Circle the letters that should be capitalized.

i have never been to disney world.

Math

37 + 90 =   7 + 4 =

18 − 9 =   17 − 8 =

What time is it?

 _____

Let's countdown 30, 29, 28, 27...

Read

"You mean," said Jimmy Skunk, "that you guess that Peter Rabbit knew that I was in that barrel, and that he jumped over it so as to make Reddy Fox run against it. Is that it?"

Sammy Jay said nothing, but winked again. Jimmy grinned. Then he looked thoughtful. "I wonder," said he slowly, "if Peter did it so as to gain time to get away from Reddy Fox."

Copy the sentence. Make sure to copy the quotation marks and capital letters. ("I wonder," said Jimmy Skunk.)

Language Arts

What does the contraction mean? Write the answer.

I'm _____   we'll _____

Math

5 + 8 =   7 + 8 =

12 – 5 =   14 – 6 =

Color the pieces to show the fraction one third. The write one third as a fraction.

Read

Jimmy Skunk ambled along down the hill. At first he was very angry as he thought of what Peter had done, and he made up his mind that Peter should be taught a lesson he would never forget. But as he ambled along, the funny side of the whole affair struck him, for Jimmy Skunk has a great sense of humor, and before he reached the bottom of the hill his anger had all gone and he was chuckling.

Copy the sentence. (Write other verbs for how Jimmy could have moved down the hill. It says he "ambled." He could have rushed, tiptoed, wandered...)

_____

_____

Language Arts

Which is the correct spelling of the plural?

try _____   fly _____

Math

8 + 3 =   67 + 40 =

15 – 7 =   11 – 4 =

How many quarters do you need to make a dollar?

Let's countdown 30, 29, 28, 27, 26, 25...

Read

So in the springtime there is always a great deal of matching of wits between the little people of the Green Forest and the Green Meadows and the Old Orchard. Those who have eggs try to keep them a secret or to build the nests that hold them where none who like to eat them can get them; and those who have an appetite for eggs try to find them.

Copy the sentence. (Those who have an appetite for eggs try to find them.)

_____

_____

_____

Language Arts

What's wrong with the sentence?

I found a coyn on the street.

Math

7 + 4 =   30 + 9 =

15 – 7 =   40 – 30 =

What's next in the pattern? Write the number.

55, 53, 51, 49, 47, 45, 43, 41, 39, 37, _____

Let's countdown 30, 29, 28, 27, 26, 25, 24...

Read

"So it's you, you black and white rascal!" he exclaimed. "I suppose you expect me to step out of your way, and I suppose I will do just that very thing. You are the most impudent and independent fellow of my acquaintance. That's what you are. You didn't get any eggs, because I gathered all of them last night. And you didn't get a chicken because they were wise enough to stay on their roosts, so I don't know as I have any quarrel with you, and I'm sure I don't want any. Come along out of there, you rascal."

Copy the sentence. ("So it's you, you black and white rascal!" he exclaimed.)

_____

_____

Language Arts

Circle the letters that should be capitalized.

my grandparents take us to pizza hut.

Math

30 + 70 =   82 + 55 =

80 − 40 =   68 − 30 =

What time is it?

_____

Let's countdown 30, 29, 28, 27, 26, 25, 24, 23...

Read

"This henhouse seems to be a very popular place. I see that the first thing for me to do after breakfast is to nail a board over that hole in the floor. So it was you, Unc' Billy Possum, who kicked that nest-egg out. Found it a little hard for your teeth, didn't you? Lost your temper and kicked it out, didn't you? That was foolish, Unc' Billy, very foolish indeed. Never lose your temper over trifles. It doesn't pay. Now I wonder what I'd better do with you."

Answer. (What does it mean to not lose your temper over trifles?)

_____

_____

Language Arts

Which are correct? Underline the two correct sentences.

Its coat is shiny.   It's raining outside.

It's eyes are blue.   Its funny how he does that.

Math

45 + 60 =   76 + 50 =

84 − 3 =   120 − 50 =

Color the pieces to show the fraction two thirds. Write the fraction.

Let's countdown 30, 29, 28, 27, 26, 25, 24, 23, 22...

Climb the Summer Slide

Read

Boats sail on the rivers,
And ships sail on the seas;
But clouds that sail across the sky
Are prettier far than these.

Rhyme the word. (Write words that rhyme with sky.)

_____

_____

Language Arts

Write the plural?

wolf _____   thief _____

Math

70 + 70 =   52 + 4 =

78 − 31 =   170 − 80 =

How much money do you have? Do you have enough to buy the toy?

72₵

Let's countdown 30, 29, 28, 27, 26, 25, 24, 23, 22, 21...

Read

There's sweetness in an apple tree,
And profit in the corn;
But lady of all beauty
Is a rose upon a thorn.

Write rhymes. (Write words that rhyme with tree and beauty.)

_____

_____

Language Arts

Which words are verbs? Underline them.

I like green eggs and ham.
I am really hungry.
They really are eager.

Math

67 + 60 =   73 + 23 =

140 – 60 =   150 – 80 =

What's next in the pattern? Write the number.

99, 88, 77, 66, 55, 44, 33, 22, _____

Read

A pin has a head, but has no hair;
A clock has a face, but no mouth there;
Needles have eyes, but they cannot see;
A fly has a trunk without lock or key.

Write rhymes. (Write words that rhyme with hair and there.)

_____

_____

Language Arts

Circle the letters that should be capitalized.

billy graham was a famous preacher.

Math

37 + 51 =   50 + 90 =

96 – 25 =   140 – 70 =

What time is it?

_____

Read

So Jimmy and Peter joined Unc' Billy, and Jimmy told the story about Old Mr. Toad all over again. Unc' Billy chuckled and laughed just as they had at the idea of Old Mr. Toad's saying he had a beautiful voice. But Unc' Billy has a shrewd little head on his shoulders. After a few minutes he stopped laughing.

Copy the sentence. (Billy has a shrewd little head on his shoulders.)

_____

_____

_____

Language Arts

What's the contraction? Write the contraction.

I am _____   she is _____

Math

$$
\begin{array}{r}
\overset{1}{2}6 \\
+\ 35 \\
\hline
61
\end{array}
\qquad
\begin{array}{r}
28 \\
+\ 34 \\
\hline
\end{array}
\qquad
\begin{array}{r}
37 \\
+\ 29 \\
\hline
\end{array}
\qquad
87 - 40 =
$$

Draw a picture that shows the fraction two thirds. Can you write the fraction?

Let's countdown 20, 19, 18...

Read

It isn't often that Peter Rabbit is truly envious, but sometimes in the joyousness of spring he is. He envies the birds because they can pour out in beautiful song the joy that is in them. The only way he can express his feelings is by kicking his long heels, jumping about, and such foolish things. While that gives Peter a great deal of satisfaction, it doesn't add to the joy of other people as do the songs of the birds, and you know to give joy to others is to add to your own joy. So there are times when Peter wishes he could sing.

Copy the sentence. (It isn't often that Peter Rabbit is truly envious.)

_____

_____

Language Arts

Write the plural?

child _____ friend _____

Math

$$47 + 24$$ $$16 + 18$$ $$16 - 7 =$$ $$60 - 30 =$$

How much money do you have? Do you have enough to buy the toy?

27¢

Let's countdown 20, 19, 18, 17...

Read

Ever since Peter Rabbit was a little chap and had first ran away from home, he had known Old Mr. Toad, and never once had Peter suspected that he could sing. Also he had thought Old Mr. Toad almost ugly-looking, and he knew that most of his neighbors thought the same way. They were fond of Old Mr. Toad, for he was always good-natured and attended strictly to his own affairs; but they liked to poke fun at him, and as for there being anything beautiful about him, such a thing never entered their heads.

Answer in a sentence. (Did Peter Rabbit believe that Mr. Toad could sing?)

_____

_____

Language Arts

How would you replace these words with a pronoun?

Joanna _____   Peter and John _____   book _____

Math

```
  53          64          150 − 80 =
+  7        + 28
```

What's next in the pattern? Write the number.

35, 40, 45, 50, 55, 60, 65, 70, 75, 80, _____

Let's countdown 20, 19, 18, 17, 16...

Read

The little stars looked down from the sky and twinkled just to see their reflections twinkle back at them from the Smiling Pool. And there and all around it was perfect peace. Jerry Muskrat swam back and forth, making little silver lines on the surface of the Smiling Pool and squeaking contentedly, for it was the hour which he loves best.

Answer the question. (What time of day is it?)

_____

Language Arts

Rewrite the proper nouns properly. What's wrong with them?

judah was a tribe of israel.

_____

Math

$$27$$
$$+\ 25$$

$$63$$
$$+\ 19$$

$$150 - 60 =$$

What time is it?

_____

Let's countdown 20, 19, 18, 17, 16, 15...

Read

The world is a wonderful great big place
And in it the young must roam
To learn what their elders have long since learned -
There's never a place like home.

Write rhymes. (Write a word that rhymes with roam and home. Write three words that rhyme with place. Get a high five and/or hug if you write more!)

_____

_____

Language Arts

Circle the subject. Underline the predicate.

We like helping others.

Math

$$28 + 15$$

$$35 + 19$$

$$140 - 60 =$$

$$17 - 8 =$$

Draw a picture to show three fifths. Can you write the fraction?

Read

Old Mother Nature doth provide
For all her children, large or small.
Her wisdom foresees all their needs
And makes provision for them all.

Write rhymes. (Write five words that rhyme with all. Write three words that rhyme with needs.)

_____

_____

Language Arts

What's wrong with the sentence? (Find five mistakes.)

have your seen what im working on.

Math

$$36 + 39$$

$$42 + 18$$

$$14 - 5 =$$

$$76 - 30 =$$

How much money do you have? Do you have enough to buy the toy?

30¢

Let's countdown 20, 19, 18, 17, 16, 15, 14, 13...

Read

Old Mr. Toad laughed right out. "Perhaps if it was, you couldn't ask so many questions," said he. "Now watch me catch that fly." His funny little tongue darted out, and the fly was gone.

Copy the sentence. ("Perhaps if it was, you couldn't ask so many questions," said he.)

_____

_____

_____

Language Arts

Write the three pronouns in the sentence you copied.

_____

Math

$$\begin{array}{r} 18 \\ + 63 \\ \hline \end{array} \qquad \begin{array}{r} 35 \\ + 27 \\ \hline \end{array} \qquad \begin{array}{r} 57 \\ - 20 \\ \hline \end{array} \qquad \begin{array}{r} 57 \\ - 25 \\ \hline \end{array}$$

What's next in the pattern? Write the number.

76, 74, 72, 70, 68, 66, 64, 62, 60, 58, _____

Let's countdown 20, 19, 18, 17, 16, 15, 14, 13, 12...

Read

Peter Rabbit didn't blame Old Mr. Toad a bit for being indignant because Peter had watched him change his suit. It wasn't a nice thing to do. Old Mr. Toad had looked very funny while he was struggling out of his old suit, and Peter just couldn't help laughing at him. But he realized that he had been very impolite, and he very meekly told Old Mr. Toad so.

Copy the sentence. (Peter Rabbit didn't blame him a bit for being indignant.)

_____

_____

Language Arts

Circle the letters that should be capitalized.

they like to eat cheerios on mondays.

Math

$$37 + 42$$

$$48 + 23$$

$$140 - 70 =$$

$$56 - 30 =$$

What time is it?

_____

Let's countdown 20, 19, 18, 17, 16, 15, 14, 13, 12, 11...

Read

Flossie, with a shake of her light curls, and a stamp of her little feet to rid them of the snow from the drift in which she had been standing, went closer to the fine-looking and intelligent dog, who did not seem to mind being all tied up with ropes and leather straps to Freddie's sled.

Write the words that show the answers. (Why do we know Flossie is a girl? Why do we know she is young? How do we know she has curly hair? How do we know it's winter?)

_____

_____

Language Arts

Circle the common nouns. Underline the proper nouns.

Europe   books   Disney   friend

Math

$$27 + 53$$

$$19 + 13$$

$$160 - 70 =$$

$$42 - 10 =$$

Draw a picture and write the fraction that shows one sixth.

Read

Snap, hearing the voice of his young master—one of his two masters by the way—wagged his tail harder than ever. Freddie made a grab for it, but missed. Flossie, seeing this, laughed and Snap, thinking it was a great joke, leaped about and barked with delight. He sprang out of the harness, which was only partly fastened on, and began leaping about in the snow. Finally he stood up on his hind legs and marched about, for Snap was a trick dog, and had once belonged to a circus.

Answer the questions. (What does it mean that Snap is a "trick" dog? How do you know? Hint: Read the rest of the sentence.)

Language Arts
What's wrong with the sentence? (Find three mistakes.)

do you heer that.

Math

74
+ 13

35
+ 25

$120 - 70 =$

$92 - 50 =$

How much money do you have? Do you have enough to buy the toy?

20¢

Let's countdown 10, 9...

Read

The dog was well enough trained so that he knew when the time for fun was over and when he had to settle down. Still wagging his tail joyously, however, Snap came up to Freddie, who started over again the work of harnessing the animal to the sled.

Copy the sentence. (Still wagging his tail joyously, Snap came up to Freddie.)

_____

_____

_____

Language Arts

Write the pronoun that would replace the phrase. Use these sentences for a little help. <u>You and I</u> went to the store. He's talking to <u>you and me</u>.

you and I _____   you and me _____

Math

$$53 + 19$$ $$35 + 36$$ $$100 - 50 =$$

$$87 - 20 =$$

What's next in the pattern? Write the number.

100, 80, 60, 40, 20, _____

Let's countdown 10, 9, 8...

Read

So Flossie held the dog's tail, while Freddie put on the harness again. This time he succeeded in getting it all arranged to suit him, and the frisky Snap was soon made fast to the sled.

"Now get on, Flossie," called her brother, "and we'll see how fast Snap can pull us."

Copy the line. ("Now get on, Flossie," he called.)

_____

_____

Language Arts

Circle the letters that should be capitalized.

on monday timothy is going to florida.

Math

19	25	120 − 40 =
+ 57	+ 48	

$$92 - 80 =$$

What time is it?

The minute hand is pointing to the 8.
The hour hand hasn't reached the 4 yet.

_____

Let's countdown 10, 9, 8, 7...

Read

"I guess so," he answered. "This harness is all busted, anyhow."

Sadly he looked at the tangled strings and straps fast to the sled, where Snap had broken away from them. The harness Freddie had made with such care was all broken now.

Copy the sentence. ("I guess so," he answered.)

_____

_____

Language Arts

Write the pronouns to replace the underlined names. <u>Phoebe and Mark</u> went to play. Give these to <u>Phoebe and Mark</u>.

_____   _____

Math

$$11 + 9$$ $$34 + 22$$ $100 - 30 =$

$28 - 10 =$

Draw a picture that shows two sevenths. Write the fraction.

Let's countdown 10, 9, 8, 7, 6...

Read

It was evident that Danny liked to play master. He could be heard giving orders to this one and the other one to get out of the way, to pull his bob around in place, and then to shove it off with its load of boys and girls.

Now, though Danny was a bully, some of the children were friendly with him for the sake of getting a ride on his sled, which was a large and expensive one.

Copy the underlined sentence. What does it mean? Hint: Read the next sentence.

_____

_____

Language Arts

What's wrong with the sentence? (Find five mistakes.)

im shor that's write

Math

$$70 + 15$$

$$69 + 12$$

$$110 - 30 =$$

$$83 - 40 =$$

How much money do you have? Do you have enough to buy the toy?

18¢

Let's countdown 10, 9, 8, 7, 6, 5...

Read

For a moment it looked as though there might be trouble, but an instant later all thoughts of it passed, for a series of girls' screams came from midway down the long hill.

All eyes were turned in that direction, and those at the top of the slope saw a team of runaway horses, attached to a heavy bobsled, plunging madly up the hill.

Copy the sentence. (A series of girls' screams came from midway down.)

_____

_____

Language Arts

Underline five pronouns. Can you find them all?

They liked it so much we gave them ours.

Math

$$9 + 43$$

$$18 + 19$$

$$120 - 90 =$$

$$87 - 70 =$$

What's next in the pattern? Write the number.

5, 10, 15, 20, 25, 30, 35, 30, 25, 20, _____

Let's countdown 10, 9, 8, 7, 6, 5, 4...

Climb the Summer Slide

Read

The day was cold, and clouds overhead seemed to tell that it was going to snow. But the young folks hoped the storm would hold off until night, when they would be safe in the big, old-fashioned farmhouse.

Everyone was well wrapped up, and Flossie and Freddie were almost lost in big rugs that had been tucked around them, for their mother did not want them to get cold.

Answer the question. (How did they know it was going to snow?)

Language Arts

Circle everything that's wrong with the sentence. (Find five things.)

peter and andrew is brotheries

Math

$$15 + 51$$

$$19 + 72$$

$$120 - 30 =$$

$$74 - 50 =$$

What time is it?

_____

Let's countdown 10, 9, 8, 7, 6, 5, 4, 3...

Read

They had brought with them the chocolate all ready to heat in a pot, and soon it was set over a fire of sticks which the boys had made on shore, scraping away the snow from the ground. Nan and Dorothy got out the packages of sandwiches and cake, and soon a merry little party was seated on the ice-boat, eating the good things.

Copy the sentence. (They had brought with them the chocolate all ready.)

_____

_____

Language Arts

Fill in the pronoun.

_____ love their new puppy.

Math

$$
\begin{array}{r} 37 \\ + 42 \\ \hline \end{array}
\qquad
\begin{array}{r} 48 \\ + 23 \\ \hline \end{array}
$$

$$140 - 70 =$$

$$56 - 30 =$$

Draw a picture that shows one fifth. Write the fraction.

Let's countdown 10, 9, 8, 7, 6, 5, 4, 3, 2...

Read

Little Bo-Peep has lost her sheep,
And can't tell where to find them;
Leave them alone, and they'll come home,
And bring their tails behind them.

Write three words that rhyme with sheep.

_____

_____

Language Arts

Finish the sentence. Make sure you end with a question mark.

How do you _____

_____

Math

9	6	4	11	14	15
+ 8	+ 7	+ 6	- 6	- 7	- 8

How much money do you have? Do you have enough to buy the toy?

     60¢

Let's countdown 10, 9, 8, 7, 6, 5, 4, 3, 2, 1!

EP provides free, complete, high quality online homeschool curriculum for children around the world. Find more of our courses and resources on our site, allinonehomeschool.com.

If you prefer offline materials, consider Genesis Curriculum which takes a book of the Bible and turns it into daily lessons in science, social studies, and language arts for your children to learn all together. The curriculum also includes learning Biblical languages. Genesis Curriculum offers Rainbow Readers and A Mind for Math, a math curriculum designed for about first through fourth grade to be done all together. Each math lesson is based on the day's Bible reading from the main curriculum. GC Steps is an offline preschool and kindergarten program. Learn more about our expanding curriculum on our site, GenesisCurriculum.com.

Made in the USA
Coppell, TX
06 April 2023

15333856R00026